The Journey

The Journey

Big Panda and Tiny Dragon

James Norbury

MANDALA

San Rafael Los Angeles London

For those on their own journey.

There was a temple high in the mountains.

Surrounded by a vast forest.

And a deep, still lake.

The temple had seen better days.

But that didn't matter
to the two friends
who made that ancient
place their home.

Big Panda and Tiny Dragon.

During the day they would travel high into the mountain peaks.

And explore the thick, tangled forests hoping to catch
a glimpse of the creatures that lived there.

At night they would watch the stars
and drink the hot tea that Tiny Dragon
so carefully prepared.

One winter evening, under a full moon,
Tiny Dragon turned to his friend and said,

"This place is incredible, Big Panda.
The trees, the mountains, the birds and the animals,
they are all so magical; we are so lucky –
so why do I feel like something is missing?

Why do I feel incomplete?"

Big Panda nodded
and took a sip of tea.

"That is a good question, little one,
and the answer is simple yet difficult.

Sleep now.

Tomorrow is a new day,
and we'll see what we can do."

Big Panda awoke early, but his friend
was already up watching the sun
rise over the mountains.

He seated himself on the rock
next to Tiny Dragon.

"You are unhappy, my little friend," said Big Panda.
"That's OK. It happens to us all.

The important thing is that you have
noticed something is wrong."

"Problems should not stop us," said Big Panda.

"They are simply nature's way of letting us
know we need to explore a different path."

"You have shared how you feel," said Big Panda.

"Sharing our lives, both the good and the bad, is what
makes us closer and lets us help each other."

"I'd help you," said Tiny Dragon,
"if you ever needed it."

"You help me every day," replied Big Panda,
"just by being yourself."

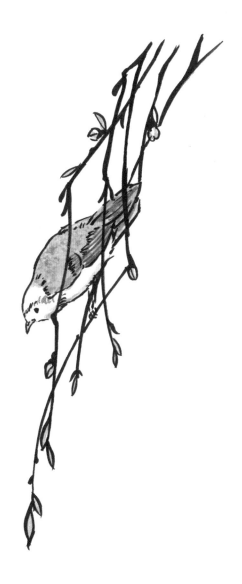

They crossed the old bridge that led to the temple's garden.

"Change," said Big Panda, "even if you don't know where it will lead,
is better than stagnation."

"In some ways, the mind is much like a garden.
It needs your care, attention and effort.

Left to its own devices it will soon become overrun with weeds.
And where there are too many weeds, flowers cannot grow."

Tiny Dragon nodded.

"But how do I pull up the weeds?"

"I will help you," said Big Panda.

"Remember, little one –
together we can do anything."

They left the garden and walked to the cliff
that overlooked the Great River.

After settling himself on the rock,
Big Panda turned to Tiny Dragon.

"We cannot just sit here and hope the
weeds will go away on their own.

We must take action.

Sometimes something needs to change,
and that requires effort.

We shall go on a journey, across the river."

They returned to the temple to close the wooden shutters
and block up the broken doorway, for it rained a lot in
the mountains and Tiny Dragon did not want his things
to get wet while they were away.

When he was finished, he placed a
few of his most-prized possessions into his little cart
and went outside to meet Big Panda.

When Big Panda saw the overstuffed cart, he slowly shook his head.

"We cannot take all of this over the river."

"But I need these things," said Tiny Dragon,
stroking his picture of Grandpa Dragon.

"Everything you need," said Big Panda,
"is already inside you."

Tiny Dragon paused – deep down
he knew Big Panda was right,
but he had one small question.

"Can I take my tea set?"

"Of course," said Big Panda.

"There is nothing wrong with enjoying the
fruits of the world, we just need to make sure
we do not lose ourselves in them."

And so Tiny Dragon clambered up onto
Big Panda's back and they followed the rocky trail
that led out of the mountains and down to the river,
leaving the old temple far behind them.

They traveled for many days through the dense forests
that covered the mountains.

They passed crashing waterfalls and dark, deep pools.

They saw colorful birds and glimpsed small deer
flitting through the towering bamboo.

Until one evening,
just as the stars were starting to come out,
they arrived at the banks of the Great River.

"We'll stop here tonight," said Big Panda.
"We can light a fire and listen to the river."

"And I will make some tea!" said Tiny Dragon.

Tiny Dragon collected some sticks and soon
water was heating over the crackling fire.

Tiny Dragon poked the fire with a stick.

"Big Panda?

I was wondering . . .

why don't I get the same pleasure collecting sticks now
that I did when I was a very tiny dragon?"

"I used to love choosing the best
sticks, brushing off the leaves and
placing them in my basket."

Big Panda thought for a moment.

"Our thoughts can lead us away from ourselves.

When you were young, the task of gathering sticks
probably took all your attention.

When you are focused in that way, your mind tends not
to wander and that creates a sense of inner stillness
from which arise feelings of joy and peace."

Tiny Dragon pondered.

"Perhaps you're right. When I was
collecting them just now, I was thinking about
whether this journey would really help.

I was not really thinking about
the sticks at all."

"Stillness is always there to be found," said Big Panda.
"And in that peace you may start to find yourself again."

Tiny Dragon felt that Big Panda was only reminding him
of something he already knew deep inside.

"And if you forget yourself,
just look up at the stars in the sky,
or listen to the pines waving in the evening breeze.

They are doing what nature intended – in this moment."

In the morning, while they were
breakfasting on bamboo and berries,
Big Panda noticed Tiny Dragon
was looking worried.

"What is it, little one?"

Tiny Dragon looked up.

"I'm afraid," he said quietly.
"I don't want to cross the river."

"It's natural to be scared," said Big Panda,
"but sometimes we must carry on anyway."

"Fear will not stop you dying,
but it may stop you from living."

They watched the sun break over dark mountains.

"Something needs to change, my little friend,"
said Big Panda.

"But if making the change was easy,
it probably wouldn't make very much difference.

Great change requires great effort."

Tiny Dragon finished his berry.
"You're right," he said.

"Crossing the river does scare me –
and so I'll be scared when I do it
– but I'm going to cross it regardless."

Together they searched the shoreline until Big Panda
found what he was looking for.

"The weather can be fierce here," he said, pointing at
some trees that had come down in a storm.

"If we use bamboo to make rope and lash together
the trunks, we'll have a raft in no time."

Despite how he felt inside,
Tiny Dragon gave a big smile
and puffed out his little chest.

"I'll get the bamboo.
You collect the logs."

By the afternoon they had built a small raft.

It was not much to look at, but it
would carry them across the river.

"I enjoyed that," said Tiny Dragon,
taking in what they had made.

"And yet," said Big Panda, "gathering bamboo
is not so different from gathering sticks.

Sometimes good and bad are just
ways of looking at the world."

As the sun was starting to set, Big Panda dragged the raft
into the shallows of the river.

They both climbed on board and Tiny Dragon used
his pole to push them off the bank.

They let the current take the raft for a while
and carry them down the river.

"This raft is a little like us,"
said Big Panda.

"Where it's been doesn't have
to determine where it's going."

"Surely the past makes a difference?"
said Tiny Dragon.

"You're right," said Big Panda, "the past is like a story that
tells us how we arrived where we are – but you can start
writing a new story right now."

Tiny Dragon fell silent and thought
about Big Panda's words.

Then from nowhere a deep rumble shook the land, and
Tiny Dragon felt spots of rain and a chilling wind.

"A storm is coming," said Big Panda, looking up at the gathering
clouds. "We should make for the shore."

But the current was stronger than it looked
and despite their efforts, they couldn't steer
the boat toward the bank.

Tiny Dragon started to panic,
but Big Panda just calmly paddled.

Aren't you scared of storms?" asked Tiny Dragon.

"Maybe once," said Big Panda, "but I've survived
them all – I've learnt that I don't need to be afraid."

Dark clouds loomed above them
and the rain fell hard and icy,
turning the surface of the river
into a ragged froth.

The raft began to spin and buck,
and the downpour had made
the wood cold, slippery and wet.

It was all Tiny Dragon could do to hold on.

Big Panda laid out flat to make himself
as stable as possible, and with a large paw,
tucked Tiny Dragon into his fur
to keep him warm and safe.

Tiny Dragon was too scared to talk.

He screwed his eyes closed
and clung on as hard as he could.

But then he suddenly remembered his tea set.

Opening one eye, he could see it lying on the raft,
the cloth wrap caught on a sharp piece of wood.

He reached out his hand to grab it, just as
the raft banged against a large rock.

The tea set broke free and tumbled into the water.

As he watched it vanish into the black, churning depths
he felt as though his heart had followed it.

What was he doing?
What was the point of all this?

He had never felt like this in his life.

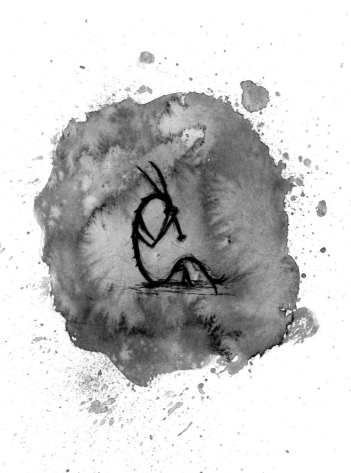

He buried his face in his hands
and sobbed.

And Big Panda heard Tiny Dragon's pain.
He wanted to help him and hold him,
and tell him it would be OK.

But he was exhausted and lacked
the strength to speak, and if he loosened
his grip, they would be washed into
the foaming waters.

All he could do was listen and
do his best to keep them safe.

Even the greatest storm will pass . . .

By morning, the storm had blown itself out.

The raft drifted aimlessly on glassy, silent waters.

Big Panda felt the sun on his back and opened his eyes.

His fur was matted with salt and his body ached, but he was reassured to feel Tiny Dragon's body curled up in his fur.

It wasn't long until his little friend awoke and crawled out into the morning air.

"We're safe!" squeaked Tiny Dragon,
and gave Big Panda a huge hug.

"But where are we?
I don't see the banks of the Great River."

"The storm raged all night," said Big Panda.
"We've been swept into the ocean."

"Oh no!" exclaimed Tiny Dragon.

"We're going to die!"

"This is not where we would
choose to be," said Big Panda,

"but it is where we are . . .

And if you try to forget about what has
happened, just for a moment,
and look around,

you might see that this is
one of the most beautiful moments
we have ever experienced."

Tiny Dragon gazed out at the endless ocean
stretching away in every direction.

"We have never been this lost," he sighed.

"If you feel lost," said Big Panda, "just close your eyes.

Hear the water lapping against the raft,

feel the sun on your skin and the breeze against your face.

There you are.

You will find yourself soon enough."

And Tiny Dragon tried . . .

But in that stillness,
all he could think of was how he had lost
his treasured tea set, how they had no food
or water and how far from home they were . . .

So he did all he could think of
and started paddling.

Hours stretched into days.

Each morning
the sun rose a burning red
over the mirror-ocean,
but there was no sign of land.

One night, Tiny Dragon,
weak from hunger and thirst,
crawled up to Big Panda
and snuggled into his fur.

"How can you be so calm?"
he asked.

"This could be the end."

Big Panda pulled Tiny Dragon in close.
"Nothing is under our control, little one . . . not really.

I just trust in life to take us where we need to be."

"But what if I'm somewhere I don't want to be?"
asked Tiny Dragon.

"That does happen," said Big Panda,
"and of course, we can try to change our
circumstances for the better,

but some situations, like this one, we cannot change
and should try to accept as they are.

That acceptance brings with it great peace."

Tired and weak, Tiny Dragon fell asleep
and Big Panda looked up at one of
the most beautiful nights he'd ever seen.

Tiny Dragon awoke with a start.

Although it was still dark,
he could see that the raft had become
beached on a sandy shore,
which gleamed white in the moonlight.

Beyond it,
high mountains rose into the night.

Tiny Dragon staggered to his feet.

"Big Panda, Big Panda! We're saved."

Big Panda opened his eyes, took in the expanse
of pale sand and the mountains beyond,
and smiled at Tiny Dragon.

"Come, little one," said Big Panda.

"Climb on my back and we'll find some food and water."

They didn't have to travel long before
they found a patch of thick grass by a winding stream.

Tiny Dragon collected some sweet red berries
and there were even some young shoots of bamboo.

They sat by the water eating, drinking and watching
the sun rise over the ocean.

"I never imagined I'd have been so grateful for food and drink,"
said Tiny Dragon, munching on a berry.

"It's funny," said Big Panda,
"how simple things, when seen with fresh eyes,
can often bring the most happiness."

Tiny Dragon nodded.

"So how far is it back to the temple?" he asked.

"I think I have learned what I needed to,
I will never take my life for granted again!"

Big Panda put a large paw on his friend's shoulder.

"We cannot go home," he said as the last star
disappeared into the dawn light.

"This is a new world, somewhere we have never been,
and somewhere from which we can never return."

"No," squeaked Tiny Dragon.

"It can't be.

We have to go home.
What about the temple,
and my things,
my friends,
and all my favourite
places . . .?

No.

We can't stay here . . .
we can't . . ."

Big Panda pointed to the
stream next to them.

"You see the way the water
travels around the rock,
Tiny Dragon?

The obstacle is there,
but the water is flowing around it,
taking the gentlest path
to its destination.

We can be the same."

Tiny Dragon looked up at
Big Panda and tried to smile,
tried to see the wisdom in his words,
but his heart was heavy.

Inside he felt he had lost everything.

He was utterly empty.

Big Panda offered a reassuring paw –
"We have gone astray, far from our home.

But . . ."

"If we have to be lost," said Big Panda,
"I am glad it's with you."

But Tiny Dragon found little comfort
in Big Panda's words.

His eyes fell to the stream,
but all he could see was the rock.

"Rain is coming," said Big Panda, looking up at a darkening sky.

"We should search for shelter."

Tiny Dragon climbed onto Big Panda's back,
and they began to ascend the mountain.

The going was hard.

There was often no path to follow, and thick, tangled roots
crawled across the forest floor.

Sometimes it was so steep that they had to find another way,
as Big Panda's paws slid and slipped in the thick mud.

Thunder cracked the sky open
and the rain fell in great sheets that
swept across the forest canopy.

"We must press on and find shelter,"
said Big Panda,
"this could continue for hours,
or even days."

But Tiny Dragon did not speak, he did not feel the rain,
he barely heard Big Panda's voice.

He felt alone and empty
in a world that meant nothing.

They journeyed for hours
until the forest gave way
to a bare expanse of rock that
rose sharply toward the
mountain's summit.

The rain was relentless,
lashing the stone and cascading
down gullies.

They struggled onward,
but there was no relief.

Just as the last of his strength was failing,
Big Panda spotted something.

"Look, Tiny Dragon,
we can shelter between those rocks."

But Tiny Dragon was silent.

Big Panda made his way carefully across the sharp,
slippery stone and managed to crawl into the cave
formed by a cluster of huge boulders.

They sat together and watched the rain,
then Big Panda turned to Tiny Dragon.

"You can talk to me, little one, if you want to."

"I make no difference to anything,"
said Tiny Dragon.

Big Panda smiled at his friend.
"You make all the difference to me."

"And I know it's hard to understand right now," said Big Panda,
"but the universe has placed us exactly where we need to be."

Tiny Dragon looked up, tears in his eyes.

"But we are hundreds of miles from home,
we don't know where we are, and we have nothing."

Big Panda took the tiny, wet dragon into his arms
and squeezed him tightly.

"That's true," he said, "and yet, somehow, we are complete."

Tiny Dragon stood up and walked out of the cave
and into the storm.

Big Panda knew he had to let him go.

Tiny Dragon walked through the downpour
with no idea where he was going.

How could he be complete?

Everything that made him who he was
had been taken away.

He had no idea how long
he had walked for,
but he was so cold and tired
he knew he had to stop.

An overhanging rock was creating the smallest
of dry patches and he staggered over to it,
dropped to the ground, and stared out
at the endless gray skies.

And then he saw it . . .

hanging from a single strand of spider silk.

A leaf . . .

It was catching just a little of the storm's dying breath,

its earthen hues catching the pale sun
as it broke through the clouds.

So delicate.

So beautiful.

The world in a moment.

Time fell away as he watched it turn.

Tiny Dragon couldn't remember seeing
anything so captivating.
So pure, perfect and delicate.

And he began to feel that the emptiness inside him
was like a cup waiting to be filled.

Filled with all the wonders the world had to offer.

There was pain, of course,
but there was so much beauty too.

"You see, don't you?"

Tiny Dragon looked around to see Big Panda,
soaked through but smiling.

"I think I do," he replied.

They watched the sun disappear behind the mountains
and as night settled over the land,
Tiny Dragon spoke for the first time in hours.

"Big Panda," he asked. "What is the universe?"

"I like to think it's our friend," said Big Panda.
"If we allow it to be."

Tiny Dragon awoke early the next morning
and although rain still swept across the mountains,

where he had previously seen hopelessness and defeat,
he now saw opportunity and beauty.

"We should be on our way," said Big Panda.
"I don't know how much longer we can last out here."

They had no food or water so they braced
themselves against the cold and the wind
and continued toward the summit.

"Look," said Tiny Dragon, "I can see the top."

And sure enough, out of the swirling mists
appeared a peak of jagged rock.

Big Panda gathered his strength
and they struggled up the last stretch.

And as they crested the final rise,
Tiny Dragon was lost for words,
for beyond, a broad river snaked its way through
a magnificent forested valley.

"This," said Big Panda,
"is where our journey has been leading us."

"And this," grinned Tiny Dragon,
"is where we will make our new home."

Hunger and cold were forgotten as Tiny Dragon sat motionless,
soaking in the beauty of what lay before him.

Eventually Big Panda tapped him on the shoulder with a large paw.

"Come," he said.

"Let's head down and find some food and water."

So the two friends made their way down into the jungle.
It was more beautiful than Tiny Dragon could have imagined.

Colorful birds in varieties he had never seen, huge plants
with flowers he could have bathed in and strange furred beasts
that crept silently through the undergrowth.

Then something caught Tiny Dragon's eye.

Half buried in the soil was a jumble of broken pottery.

After a little digging,
Tiny Dragon found a round pot
and two mismatched, chipped little cups.

"Come on," he said, picking a few choice buds off a bush.

"I recognize these leaves – they make delicious tea.
Let's celebrate."

They seated themselves under the boughs
of an ancient, twisted tree
and Tiny Dragon prepared a small fire.

"What are we celebrating?" asked Big Panda.

"Us . . ." said Tiny Dragon. "It's been a long journey with many challenges and we're both still here – that seems a good reason to me."

"You know," said Tiny Dragon,
"I think this is the best tea set I've ever had."

"Why is that?" asked Big Panda.

"Because it's the one I have now."

Tiny Dragon packed up his tea set in a huge leaf,
and they picked their way along winding animal trails
and over dark, gurgling streams.

"How are you feeling, little one?"
asked Big Panda.

Tiny Dragon thought for a moment.

"I still feel some sadness at the loss of my friends,
my home and, of course, my tea set, but I think maybe
I am learning to be more accepting of things."

"It seems that the more I unclench my hand," said Tiny Dragon,
"the more the world seems to place into it."

"I have come to realize that it's not always
the situation that is making me unhappy,
but the way I think about it.

The less I try to control the world,
the freer I am to watch it play out in all its untamed wonder."

Big Panda nodded his
head in understanding.

But despite having learnt
so much, Tiny Dragon couldn't
stop his mind occasionally wandering
back to all the things he would never see again.

"How are you so wise, Big Panda?"

Big Panda paused for a moment.

"We all have wisdom inside us, my little friend, but it's a very quiet, gentle voice, so you might need to be very still to hear it."

"But you always seem to know the answers," said Tiny Dragon.

Big Panda grinned.

"Well, I have made a lot more mistakes than you."

Then, just as they were thinking about stopping for the day,
they saw what looked like a structure in the distance.

As they moved closer, they could see it was an ancient
temple overgrown with trees and plants.

There were no signs of past occupants,
and aside from a few monkeys and birds,
no one seemed to pay them very much attention.

Big Panda checked inside and it seemed safe and sheltered.

"I think we may have found our new home."

That night, they sat in the shadows of the ruined temple and drank tea made from spring water and fresh green buds.

"I don't think the world will ever be quite the way I want it to be," said Tiny Dragon, "and some things I can never change.

But I think maybe *I* have changed, so that those things that I couldn't accept before – I am starting to be OK with."

"I feel a bit like this cup," said Tiny Dragon.

"I've been through a tough time
and I feel like I've been damaged.

But these little cracks," he said,
holding the cup up to the moon,
"are what let the light shine through."

Tiny Dragon poured his friend another cup of tea
and sat down next to him.

"Thank you," he said, stroking the big bear's head.

"What for?" asked Big Panda.

"I went wrong so many times, and every time you were there for me.
You never judged me, left me or scolded me.

I hope this time I've got it right."

Big Panda hugged the little dragon.

"As long as we're alive," said Big Panda,
"we will keep making mistakes and end up getting lost;
that is the nature of things.

But as long as we're both here,
we'll keep helping each other and we will find our way."

That night Big Panda and Tiny Dragon slept deeply, their tired, aching bodies rested safely in the ruins of the old temple.

And as dawn broke across the mountains, they were greeted by the most magnificent sunrise heralding a new day and a new beginning.

"There are so many unknowns and possibilities out there,"
said Tiny Dragon.

"Well then," said Big Panda, "let's see how many we can try."

The End . . .

of this journey.

Afterword

The Journey of *The Journey*

The original Big Panda and Tiny Dragon book was a compilation of individual drawings and dialogue that I created with the intent of sharing them on the internet. Although this created pictures which were very concise and immediate, they left me no way to explore a longer narrative.

In this second book, I have been able to tell a tale and that is one of the things I love the most.

I have always been attracted by the idea of a journey wherein the traveler struggles with both the environment and themselves. And although we tend to want our protagonist to succeed, I don't personally feel that success should be absolute. Life is not often like that and in a book like this I tried hard to avoid a happily-ever-after ending, thereby making it more relatable to the reader.

Yes, the characters do end up finding somewhere new to live and Tiny Dragon has discovered things about himself which will allow him to weather life's storm more easily, but they have both lost a great deal; they can never go home, they can never see their friends again and they are strangers in a strange land with all the fears and dangers that entails.

The story essentially begins with change (Tiny Dragon's discontent) and ends with change (a new home in a new place). Both of these changes are scary, but both could be considered necessary to move through life and become less fearful and more content.

When I first set out to create the book, I decided to base it on the idea of a spiritual journey which starts not simply with discontent, but the acknowledgment of that discontent and the desire to do something about it. The protagonists then go on a journey of ups and downs – one minute things are looking up, then another disaster, then some light at the end of the tunnel, which is swiftly snuffed out. I feel personally this reflects my own experience and that of others I know, which I hope adds a bedrock of authenticity to the tale.

This led to a strange series of experiences where I often found myself so immersed in the process of expressing the character's emotional journey that my own feelings would begin to mirror those of Tiny Dragon and sometimes even Big Panda. Perhaps this is because their story is, in many ways, a retelling of my own.

I purposefully kept the book simple with only two characters. The scenery tends to mirror Tiny Dragon's mind state, where the bleaker he feels, the more barren the world becomes. I have endeavored to always make the world appear beautiful (because it is), but our little hero's perception of that world fluctuates, and I have tried to make the reader's experience mirror that.

Other aesthetic choices I have made include having the character generally move from left to right when things are progressing, and right to left when things are falling apart. I also changed to a completely different paint palette when the characters land in the new world to instill a subtle sense that everything is different.

I have also used, toward the front of the book, a Torii arch, which is a structure typically found on the way into Japanese Shinto temples and which represents the passage from the everyday material world into the more sacred, spiritual one.

It is my sincere hope that this story speaks to your heart and that if you find some of Tiny Dragon's struggle relatable, you might find some solace in the idea that change, albeit a little scary, is possible and with patience, can lead to better things.

MANDALA

An Imprint of MandalaEarth
PO Box 3088
San Rafael, CA 94912
www.MandalaEarth.com

Find us on Facebook: www.facebook.com/MandalaEarth
Follow us on Twitter: @MandalaEarth

First published in Great Britain by Michael Joseph
Text © 2022 James Norbury
Illustrations © 2022 James Norbury
The author has asserted his moral rights

ISBN: 978-1-64722-973-3

CEO: Raoul Goff
Publisher: Roger Shaw
VP of Manufacturing: Alix Nicholaeff
Art Director: Ashley Quackenbush
Editorial Director: Katie Killebrew
Editorial Assistant: Amanda Nelson
Senior Production Manager: Joshua Smith
Senior Production Manager, Subsidiary Rights: Lina s Palma-Temena

ROOTS of PEACE   REPLANTED PAPER

Mandala Publishing, in association with Roots of Peace, will plant two trees for each tree used in the manufacturing of this book. Roots of Peace is an internationally renowned humanitarian organization dedicated to eradicating land mines worldwide and converting war-torn lands into productive farms and wildlife habitats. Roots of Peace will plant two million fruit and nut trees in Afghanistan and provide farmers there with the skills and support necessary for sustainable land use.

Manufactured in China by Insight Editions

10 9 8 7 6 5 4 3

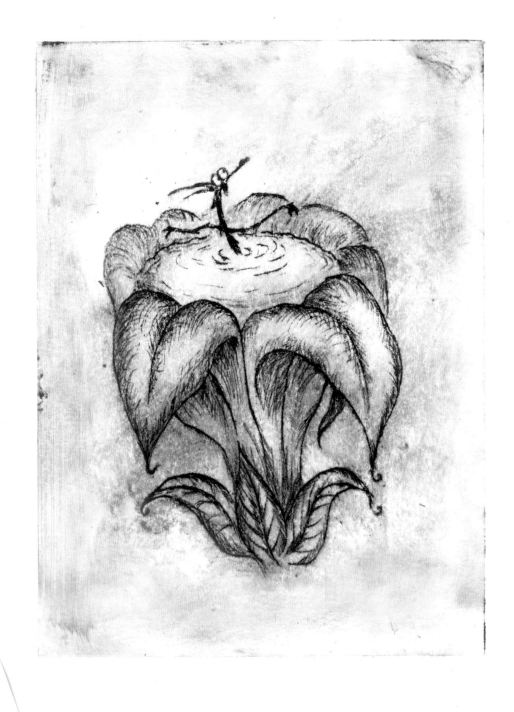

WOMEN